Farm Anim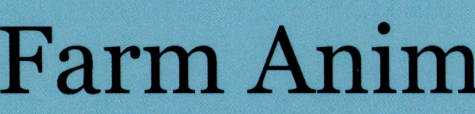

Kids Book

Billy Grinslott

Kinsey Marie Books

ISBN - 9781957881850

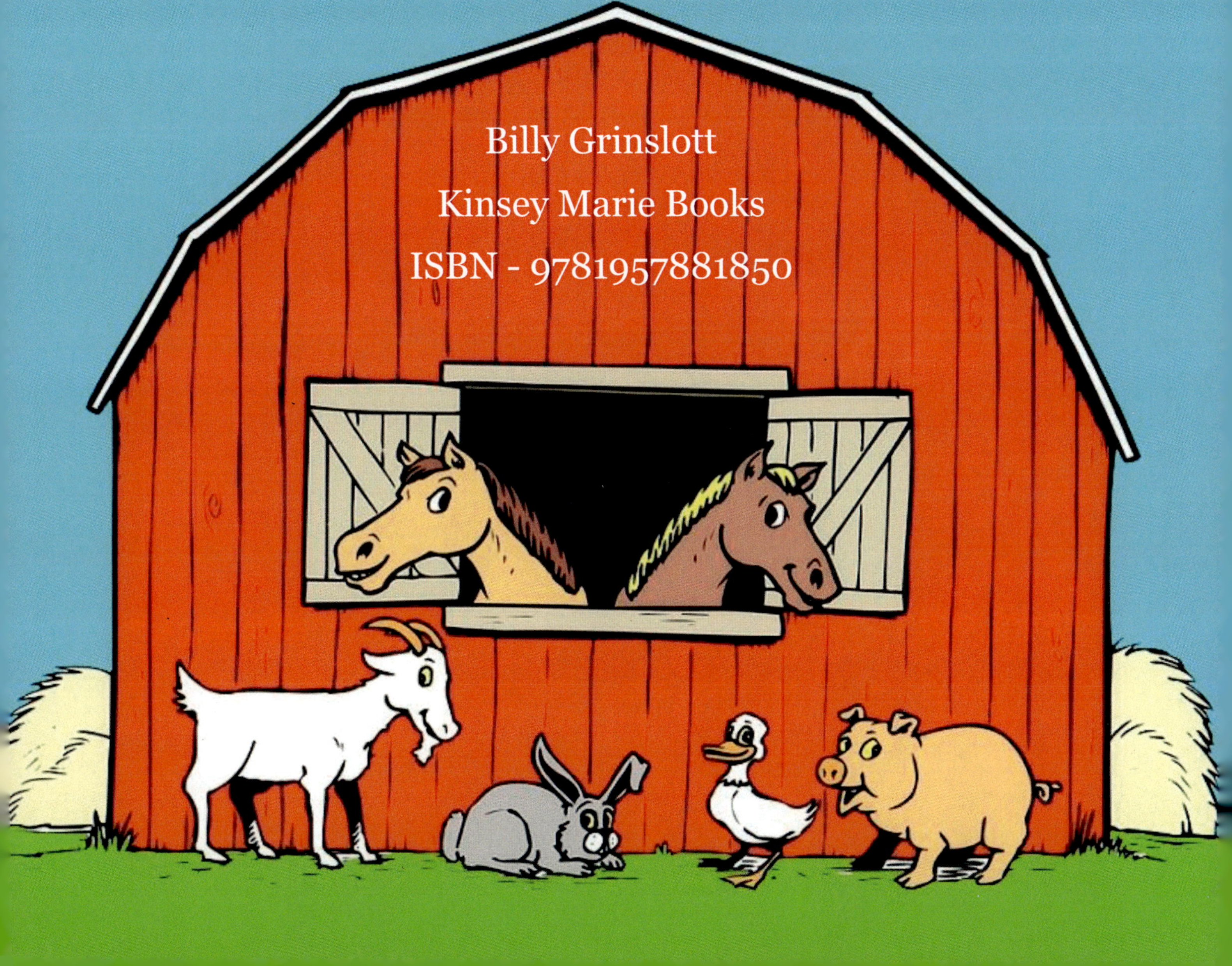

Cock-a-doodle-do. Chickens are the most raised bird on a farm. Male chickens, Roosters wake up every morning and make a loud crowing noise that can be heard for miles. Hens, female chickens lay eggs daily and they are collected and sold to stores for us to eat. Chickens have great memories & can recognize over 100 faces. Chickens can see in color. They dream when they sleep. Chickens have been around since the dinosaur days.

Quack, Quack. Many farms have ducks that live on the farm. City ducks have a different quack than country ducks. Ducklings communicate with each other before hatching. Ducks have great eyes. Ducks can move each eye independently and they store information on the opposite sides of their brain. Ducks can sleep with one eye open to watch for other animals. Ducks have a favorite color. According to research, ducks may show a preference for colors in the green or blue spectrum.

Honk, honk. Goose is the term for female geese, male geese are called ganders. A group of geese on land or in water are a gaggle. Many farms have geese, they are raised like chickens for their meat or eggs. Male geese protect the nest while the female geese sit on the eggs. They are the largest waterfowls, the other being swans.

oh-OH, oh-OH. Swans are huge. Trumpeter swans are the largest native waterfowl and the heaviest flying birds in North America. Many farms don't raise swans anymore due to regulations. But you can still see them swimming in nearby ponds, lakes and feeding with chickens and other livestock.

Coo, Coo. Pigeons are abundant and easy to see on farms. Many pigeons live in barns and are the most common bird you will see flying around the farm. Pigeons may have been the first domesticated bird. Pigeons are navigation experts and were once used to carry messages to other people so they could communicate with each other.

Gobble, Gobble. Turkeys were once primarily raised for their feathers. An adult turkey has around 6 thousand feathers and they were used for insulation in jackets. Male turkeys are called toms or gobblers. Female turkeys don't gobble, but they do make a purring noise.

Grunt, grunt. There are approximately 1,500 emu farms and roughly 11,500 emus in the U.S. Some farmers see the birds as beneficial because they eat the burrs that entangle sheep wool as well as caterpillars and grasshoppers which eat crops.

Chirp, chirp. There are only a few hundred ostrich farms in the US. Ostriches don't fly even though they have wings. They are the fastest runners of any birds or other two-legged animal. They have very strong legs. They bury their eggs in a whole and can be seen putting their head into the hole to check their eggs.

There are several mink farms. Minks are great at burrowing and building tunnels. They're also very skilled climbers and swimmers. They prefer to keep to themselves. They have great hearing. Mink babies are known as kits or kittens. Mink purr when they're happy, just like cats.

Many farms raise and sell rabbits. A baby rabbit is called a kit, a female is called a doe and a male is called a buck. Rabbits are very social and like to live in groups. A rabbit's teeth never stop growing. Rabbits perform an athletic leap, known as a binky, when they're happy, performing twists and kicks in midair. They make great pets.

Humm, Humm. There are about 53,000 alpacas on farms in the USA. Alpacas are raised for their fleece coat, just like sheep. Alpacas are known for spitting, but they usually don't. They are related to llamas. Alpacas are very quiet and gentle animals. Unlike most livestock, alpacas are clean and easy to care for. Considering they do not have an awful or strong smell, it makes sense why more people have them as pets than other types of livestock.

Baa, baa. Sheep have a wool fur coat. Farmers will shave sheep and collect the wool to make clothing. Many clothes are made from the wool collected from sheep's fur. Their wool fur coat regrows forever so they can be shaven multiple times. Sheep are smart and can recognize up to 50 other sheep faces and remember them for two years. A baby sheep is called a lamb. If a sheep falls on it's back, it can't turn over to stand up again. They have nearly 360-degree vision.

There are over 2 million Zebu in the US. Zebus are a type of cattle, just like cows. Zebus can also be milked just like cows. Zebus are one of the oldest breeds of cattle in the world. There are 75 different species of zebu. Unlike cows they have humps on their backs.

Llamas are known for spitting at other animals and even humans. One fourth of the llamas in the U.S. live in Oregon. Llamas are excellent guardians. They keep coyotes and other sheep-hungry dogs at bay. Llamas have sharp eyes and ears and are quite intelligent. They can spot a troublesome meddler before people do and will often charge a predator in groups to scare them away.

Most of the Dromedary camels in the US live on Amish and Mennonite farms. They raise and sell the camels to other farmers. They also lease them to zoos and churches, which use them for nativity scenes. They can go for weeks without drinking water. They store fat in parts of their bodies known as humps. The humps act as heat regulators for camels to keep them cool. Camel milk is among the healthiest milk in the world.

Yaks are now on ranches in more than a dozen states. Yaks prefer to live in higher altitudes where its cooler. Like cows, the yak has more than one stomach. They have long fur and in winter a yak can survive temperatures as low as minus 40 degrees C. At night and in snowstorms they will protect themselves from the cold by huddling up together with their calves in the warmer center.

Elk farming has become very popular. The male elk is the loudest member of the deer family. They have a bugling call that is unique. Elk are nocturnal animals, they are primarily active during the night. They prefer to live in colder areas and in the mountains. They are social animals. Elk live in large groups, also called herds, that can reach well into the hundreds.

Relatively unknown, there are small water buffalo farms all over the United States. Some dairy farms supply area restaurants with buffalo milk. Because water buffalo milk has a higher butterfat content than cow's milk, it doesn't have to be mixed with as much cow's cream to make gelato. Buffalo milk is the core contributing factor to producing ice cream that's rich in flavor and its creamy texture feels smooth and velvety on the tongue when you taste it.

There are only a few reindeer farms in the lower US states and some in Alaska. Reindeer and caribou are the same animal and are a member of the deer family. Both male and female reindeer grow antlers, while in most other deer species, only the males have antlers.

Oink, Oink. Pigs are raised all over the world, and provide valuable products to humans, including pork, lard, leather, glue, fertilizer, and medicines. Pigs like to lay in mud because they can't sweat like humans, so they lay in the mud to cool off. Pigs are clean animals, and they are smarter than dogs. Mother pigs sing to their babies. Pigs dream and like to sleep nose-to-nose. They are very social and love it when you rub their belly.

Moo, Moo. Female cows provide us with milk. Dairy farms raise many female cows for their milk. Milk has lots of nutrients and vitamins. Cows have a visual field of 330° almost an all-around view. Cows don't need much sleep and can take a nap while standing up. They are very social and like hanging out in groups.

Bison are also known as the American buffalo. Bison are the largest mammal in North America. A bison's hump is composed of muscle. They can run up to 35 miles per hour. They're extremely agile. Bison can spin around quickly, jump high fences and are strong swimmers. They have thick fur and can withstand very cold temperatures. Bison have long fur and buffalo do not. Can you tell the difference?

Baa, baa. There are several types of goats on a farm, but the Billy goat has a memorable name. Goats were one of the first animals to be tamed by humans. Goats don't have teeth on their upper jaw. Goats have rectangular pupils. They have 4 stomachs. Goats have incredible agility and balance. Cashmere coats come from goats. Goats milk is the most popular milk worldwide.

Farming of white-tailed deer has become a successful in the United States, with more than 4,000 operations. White-tailed deer have good eyesight and hearing. Only male deer grow antlers, which are shed each year. A young deer is called a fawn. An adult male deer is called a buck. The female is called a doe.

Hee-haw, Hee-haw. Donkeys have long been used as pack animals to carry loads and for draft work in agriculture pulling heavy loads. They make great pasture pets, as a guardian for livestock and sometimes as a companion for horses. Donkeys are very strong and intelligent. A donkey is stronger than a horse of the same size. Donkeys have an incredible memory. They can recognize areas and other donkeys they were with for up to 25 years.

Eeyore, Eeyore. Mules are by far one of the strongest animals for their size. Farmers, ranchers, and outdoorsman use them to carry heavy loads. Mules tend to be healthier, sounder and live longer than horses. Mules are less prone to injuries because they've got good senses on steep terrain.

The principal use of beef cattle is meat production. Other uses include leather, and beef by-products used in candy, shampoo, cosmetics, and insulin. One cowhide can make 18 soccer balls or 20 footballs. Beef cattle are raised in all 50 states of the US. But there are more cattle in 9 states in the US than there are people living there. The United States and Brazil have the most beef cattle in the world.

Neigh, neigh. Besides riding, horses are used for pulling things and for rounding up livestock. Horses were one of the first animals people used for riding on. Horses can't breathe through their mouth. Horses can sleep standing up. Horses have a nearly 360-degree field of vision. Horses do not have teeth in the middle of their mouth. Horses are highly intelligent animals. There are over 600 types of horses. They are good pets.

Meow, Meow, Meow. You will most likely see many cats on a farm. Cats help farmers by keeping control of the pests on the farm, like mice and other rodents. They are sometimes called barn cats, because they live in the barn to help control rodent populations. Which would otherwise eat or contaminate crops, especially grain or feed for other livestock. They have an important job to do around the farm.

Ruff, Ruff, Ruff. Most farms will have pet dogs. The dogs are there to help keep other animals away from the livestock. Many farmers use dogs to help round up cattle and sheep. They are trained to herd up the animals and move them to where the farmer wants them to be. In past times they used dogs to herd cattle into town, so they could be sold at the market for food. Dogs are loyal and make great pets.

The End

Thanks

Author Page
Farm Animals
Billy Grinslott and Kinsey Marie Books

Thanks for Reading

ISBN - 9781957881850

Copyright, All Rights Reserved

Made in the USA
Middletown, DE
17 March 2024